PERSONAL ~~ ~~

FOR

BEGINNERS & DUMMIES

MANAGING YOUR MONEY

BY: GIOVANNI RIGTERS

Copyright © 2019

Table of Contents

Important Disclaimer *4*

Introduction *5*

Chapter 1: Introduction to Personal Finance *7*

Chapter 2: Personal Budgeting *12*

Chapter 3: Personal Income and Spending *18*

Chapter 4: Personal Lifestyle Debt *20*

Chapter 5: Investing and Trading *27*

Chapter 6: Insurance Coverage *38*

Chapter 7: Retirement Planning *47*

Conclusion *53*

Important Disclaimer

Please note the information contained within this document is for educational and entertainment purposes only. All effort has been executed to present accurate, up to date, and reliable, complete information. No warranties of any kind are declared or implied. Readers acknowledge that the author is not engaging in the rendering of legal, financial, medical, or professional advice. The content within this book has been derived from various sources. Please consult a licensed professional before attempting any techniques outlined in this book.

By reading this document, the reader agrees that under no circumstances is the author responsible for any losses, direct or indirect, which are incurred as a result of the use of the information contained within this document, including, but not limited to, — errors, omissions, or inaccuracies.

Introduction

You can quickly lose all your income if you are unable to create a concrete plan to guide you on spending. This is a simple fact.

Every one of us has been at that point where our income doesn't match our expenses. To meet your expenses, you may take on an additional job to earn more money. If you're still in this situation, have you sat down to review your habits?

You can continually look for ways to successfully grow your income. But if you keep growing your lifestyle along with it, then you will find yourself in the same position. It is a mistake to try to achieve a different result with the same actions.

Personal finance management is the key to creating the breakthrough you need in your finances. It covers all areas, including your spending, income, investing, and savings, to ensure you live a better life. Adopting the strategies of personal money management is crucial in getting rid of your bad spending habits, identifying and monitoring your expenses, creating a budget, and sticking with it, and many more.

In this book, you will learn about personal money management and other lifestyle changes that can be beneficial to the process. The minimalist lifestyle is one of these lifestyle changes. Being a minimalist is an excellent way to spend less while living a comfortable life.

As you progress, you will find tips on how to save more money and reduce your expenses by performing some actions that are very simple to implement.

Chapter 1: Introduction to Personal Finance

Personal Finance requires identifying your expenses which is essential if you want to take charge of your finances. It is a simple way to avoid the feeling of working so hard with no tangible asset to show for your work. When you want to understand your money management habits better, this is the first action you must take. Through the process, you can identify various issues regarding how you spend money and make a conscious effort to change them.

Spending Habits You Need to Change

Some spending habits are not suitable for you, and you need to change them as quickly as possible. To make these changes, you first must identify the patterns. If you're unsure of what practices are bad for you, here are a few you need to change:

Impulse Spending

If you want to save money, avoid buying on impulse because it will cost you money down the line. The problem with impulse spending is the inability to track your expenses due to the possibility of mixing these purchases with your necessities.

There are different reasons why this may happen. If you go shopping for essential items and you happen to find a good deal, it is common for these deals to get your attention. You consider the amount you will save and decide to purchase this item. Since you didn't include it in your budget, it becomes impulse spending regardless of the money it saves you.

Gambling
This is one of the few activities that are usually not worth all the money you spend. Betting can quickly become a habit or addiction in your life. This addiction doesn't add anything positive since it usually leads to excessive loss of money. It doesn't matter if it is something as familiar as buying lottery tickets.

Occasional gambling, when you are out on vacation to places like Las Vegas, usually doesn't count. It becomes a problem if you find it challenging to avoid gambling activities like poker. The worst case is if you are on a losing streak despite this addiction. You put yourself at risk of losing your job, home, and family if you don't rethink your actions.

Missing Your Credit Card Payments
Credit cards put a strain on your finances, depending on how you use them. These cards were intended to promote a good life for individuals, but they are steadily becoming a cause for concern. Your problems with a credit card will become noticeable as soon as you miss a payment.

A simple way to quickly understand the effect of a credit card on your finances is to review your monthly statements. Through this review, you will find information on the minimum amount you should pay if you want to clear off your debt by a particular year, your interest payments for a specific month, and the duration of the repayment when you focus on minimum payments.

Carefully reviewing the statement shows that the minimum payment option doesn't offer the chance to progress significantly. You will be paying off the interest for many years to come.

Developing New Habits

As you take steps to change your bad spending habits, you need to create new habits that will improve your spending. This section will introduce some practices that you can adopt to spend money the right way.

Do Your Research Before Spending?

For anyone that wants to make sure they are spending their money on the right things, researching before a purchase is crucial. Research on the product will expose its features and defects. You also identify areas where the product doesn't meet your requirements.

Through research, you can learn about some of the perks that you receive from the manufacturer when you purchase the product. Price comparison online is another benefit of the research that can lower the cost of purchase.

Avoid Eating Out

These restaurants are running a business. They need to pay their staff and purchase inventory, so they inflate the price of meals so they can make a profit.

While it is cheaper to cook at home, you think about the convenience and may say it is worth it. However, it isn't worth the cost.

Not only do you save money, but you also eat healthier when you cook meals at home.

Negotiating Bills
The markets are saturated with lots of companies competing to get you to become a loyal customer. You can use this competition to your benefit and leverage it as a tool in negotiating for a reduction in expenses.

This is especially useful if you are considering becoming a new customer. The approach you take for a successful negotiation will differ from one company to the other. Understanding what works for the company you are currently dealing with is essential.

Do your research, know your credit score, and have a clear idea of your financial position so you can provide facts that make it difficult for them to decline your request. Compare the current price you are paying with what is available on other platforms to determine the most expensive of these options.

Control Your Utility Use
Your utility bills will vary from one month to the next, and your payment can be higher if you don't learn the proper methods of utilization. There are simple habits you need to change if you want to minimize your utility expenses.

Turning off your electronics, turning off lights, opening the windows, sun drying your clothes, and unplugging devices can help in utility conservation. In addition to saving you money, these habits also assist in environmental protection efforts.

You will learn more about these steps in a later chapter.

Compare Prices for Major Purchases
When shopping for large items, try to ensure you are paying the lowest price for the same value. Different shops will offer the same product at varying amounts, depending on how much they are adding as their profit. As a business, no one wants to run at a loss.

You can save money and make a more informed decision when you take the time to compare multiple prices. The additional money you save when you purchase an item for less should go toward increasing your savings and should not be used for discretionary expenses.

Some individuals create a spreadsheet on which they can include the price of the item from different stores for easy comparison and read reviews from other customers.

We all have spending habits that we adopt because we think they can improve our finances. It is crucial to learn more about a spending habit before implementing it in your life. Certain practices seem good on the surface but have a negative result.

Chapter 2: Personal Budgeting

Budgeting is crucial to help you keep track of your expenses and income. First, you need to obtain a bank statement of your income and payments from your financial institution. This statement will clearly show you a list of your expenses against your income. Your current lifestyle is similar to the nature of your bank statement. You should pay close attention to your spending trends while comparing the expenditure to your level of income.

Does your list of expenses match your income? Does your expense column exceed your income column? You should scrutinize this information to understand your level of fiscal responsibility. What are your primary sources of income? Are those income sources regular or steady? What are the periods between income entries? What are the periods between expenditure entries? All this information will give you a current state of your money flow status.

You can use this status as a basis for making positive alterations to your budget for your future financial security. Once you develop the habit of preparing budgets, you will always keep track of your finances and your money movements up until your retirement. Even when you will cease to receive your regular income due to retirement, your budget-making skills will pull you through this period with alternate sources of revenue.

During retirement, cash flow will be tight, and you will have developed the self-discipline in limiting your expenses to only what is necessary. Budget preparation and respecting it is a skill which, when learned early enough, will keep you financially responsible and independent well into your golden years.

Save Often
When keeping track of your income and expenditure during budgeting, your savings or lack thereof will be well visible. This information is so obvious that it immediately catches your eye before you have the time to scrutinize the other details. Financial budgeting and savings estimation are exercises that typically go hand in hand. Your savings is the number you have left after eliminating all the necessary expenses.

In simple terms, it is what you make or earn, minus what you spend. However, in everyday life, this straight forward picture does not often correspond to reality. Just like anyone else, in real life, you are bound to encounter unforeseen expenses or unexpected financial commitments that are unavoidable and unpredictable. Hence, your savings will vary from time to time. You must maximize your savings over time to enable you to face life's unexpected challenges. Once again, using your bank statement, you should pay attention to your recurrent expenditures.

Ask yourself: "Are the expenses essential to your survival or well-being?" Your essentials are the needs that you cannot do without such as food, mortgage repayments, transportation, rent. As the name suggests, recurrent expenditures are the ones that you need to take care of on specified regular intervals. These intervals could be weekly, monthly, or yearly—and these expenses are typical of your subscriptions. Now study the non-essential outgoings such as unnecessary pairs of shoes, gym memberships, and cable subscriptions.

These expenses are examples of what you do not need to survive. Get rid of such non-essential costs, and once you have made it a habit to live without them, you will undoubtedly increase your savings margin. Now, imagine making this selection every year and accumulating your savings over time up until your retirement. In the end, you will have accumulated a relatively healthy financial nest egg to sustain you further comfortably.

Get Out of Debt
You must learn to be fiscally responsible and spend under what you can afford. The best way you can avoid debt is by practicing sound and responsible management of your finances. This system goes back to making a proper financial plan and sticking to it, i.e., by putting budgeting into practice. When you veer off your budgetary limits, you become exposed to debt opportunities. If not properly managed, you may spiral deeper into more debt and end up in a debt trap or, even worse, in bankruptcy.

You should learn as early in your financial life as possible that debt is a disastrous liability to have. You should avoid debt at all costs. However, if you cannot prevent it in any way, then you should strive to settle debts promptly at the earliest opportunity. A liability is a loan, and the debtor will treat it as a commodity, which he will lend to you. However, the unique trait of this so-called commodity is that it comes with a penalty. When you return the product to the lender, he will expect an extra cost to accompany it. This additional cost is what is defined "interest." Therefore, you should understand that loans attract financial investment, and this interest is what makes loans dangerous.

You will inevitably end up paying back more than you initially took on as debt. While you are still young, employed, and getting a steady source of income, there is usually a temptation to engage in risky financial behaviors such as gambling. These temptations lure you with promises of profitable returns from small amounts of your money. In the end, you invariably lose your money and start relying on debt to get by. Gambling is a speculative financial activity based on probability. Most people get into debt traps through their excessive gambling habits.

As a prudent personal financial manager, you need to stay away from gambling opportunities, regardless of how tempting they may be. Credit cards execute your expenses on debt, so you need to get into the habit of paying using either debit cards or cash for this specific reason. In this manner, you will not risk spending what you do not have. Always remember that the greater the debt you accumulate is, the harder it becomes to pay it off. As the saying goes, debt begets more debt.

To settle your debt, you will need a second debt— and to solve that second one, you will need additional liability and so on. In all these instances, the amount of interest multiplies, and, in the end, you may end up paying up more in accumulated interest than the actual original debt.

As you get older and approach your retirement, you begin to realize how your careless financial management habits and endless debts eventually catch up to you. Be aware that after employment, you will not have that steady source of income that you once took for granted. Your financial needs will still be present, but your source of financial support will be non-existent.

No savings or investments means no nest egg to rely on in retirement. The living standard that you used to enjoy earlier in debt is suddenly not available anymore. Retirement homes and medical costs become expenses that you cannot afford. You become more likely to end up homeless in old age after your retirement. To avoid regrets from your earlier lifestyle of debt, you should learn how to be prudent with your money.

You should invest your finances for a better future in retirement. If you do not, then when retired, you will have nothing left for your years of employment. You end up suffering more in retirement than during your work.

Check Your Spending Every month
Are you sticking to your budget? If not, where are you going astray, and how can you fix that? Take a look at your spending every month and compare it to your budget worksheet to see how things are going.

Budgeting can be challenging if you have not developed it into a habit. You need to make hard choices every day to implement your plan properly. You will be declining offers from friends to eat out or to buy more than one bottle of beer after work. The hardest challenge of all is to resist old habits that may be causing our financial problems.

In the beginning, you need to find ways to motivate yourself into budgeting. You need to have an excellent reason to save money. You should think of your reason for becoming efficient with your money. You need to examine your situation and ask yourself why you need to start budgeting.

Track Your Spending

Ok, so this doesn't exactly sound like buckets of fun. I know. But think, there's a reason why every successful business tracks their expenses. Don't they have a hope in hell of controlling them if they have no idea what they are in the first place, right? Similarly, treat your finances, and you'll be well on your way to having your finances function as a well-run, profitable business. Knowledge is power, my friend — arm yourself with as much knowledge about where your money is going as you possibly can!

Track Your Income

Well, this one is certainly more fun than step one, and equally important! Tracking your income will give you a maximum baseline level for your expenses. Knowing this number will go a long way to helping you to stay out of bad debt, and making yourself a future that is as worry-free as possible, as far as your finances are concerned.

Have an Emergency Fund

Now I know that right now, you're living paycheck to paycheck, and figuring out how to save up an emergency fund seems impossible. But I'd be letting you down if I didn't at least plant the idea of it into your mind — because once you implement the strategies you'll learn in this book and stop living paycheck to paycheck, you'll have the breathing room you need to figure out how to amass an emergency stash of cash. Sound good? As you know, there is no quicker way to skewer a budget than to have an expensive emergency crop up that puts you into a huge pile of unwanted debt. Imagine the peace of mind you'd enjoy if you had an emergency fund that you'd saved up ahead of time.

How much less stress would you have in your life if you knew without a doubt that if you lost your job, you could survive (and thrive) just fine for six months or more, coasting on your savings?

Experts often recommend establishing an emergency fund that could sustain all of your financial needs for a minimum of six months. And remember, if this seems impossible, please don't worry. It's okay if you don't have this kind of money right now. Just keep in mind that not having the money right now does not mean you won't have the money later on.

You now know some of the most powerful things you can do to take control of your money. All of those things will be accounted for as you go through the process of making your budget. But first, it would be a good idea to arm you with a motivation booster.

Chapter 4: Personal Lifestyle Debt

Dealing with Credit Card Debt

With the above strategies to pay off your debt, you can implement the following to help with your credit card debts. These are effective strategies that are easy to apply. They include the following:

Balance Transfer Cards

Interest rate is one thing that comes from using credit cards. With some interest rates being up to 17%, the interest you pay at the end of the repayment period will be substantial.

For a duration, a balance transfer card offers individuals a 0% APR. For example, on a 15-month term, there will be no interest on your debt for this period. This provides an opportunity for individuals to pay off their debts with ease.

Depending on your commitment to debt repayment, you can clear off your debt during the introductory period. Those who still have a balance after this period will need to pay interest. So how do you take advantage of the balance transfer method?

If you have a high-interest credit card, then you need to search for a balance transfer card. Once you find a suitable card, then you can transfer your balance from your old card to the new card if you are approved. The process is very straightforward.

Despite the ease of use, you must note that you will pay a transfer fee. The value of the payment may be a percentage of the transfer amount or a set figure, depending on which is higher. You must read the rules of the balance transfer card since there will be information on how the introductory period applies and any possible increase in interest rate.

Using a Personal Loan
Another standard method many people adopt to pay off credit card debt includes the use of a personal loan. You can use this for other forms of debt, but there is a reason this is not advisable, and we will discuss this later. There are reasons people still use this option.

Debt consolidation is one reason people use this option. To make it easy to track their debts, they consolidate multiple credit card debts into a single debt. If they can avoid adding additional debt, they can more easily focus on paying off this debt.

Reducing the interest rate on their debts is another significant reason to take out a personal loan. This means searching for a personal loan with an interest rate that is much lower than their credit card debts. If the personal loan doesn't reduce the interest rate on your debts, it isn't your best option.

Now that your debts are now combined into one, it is possible to reduce the monthly repayment. A quick comparison will show that the total minimum payments on multiple credit card debts are higher than the minimum amount on a single personal loan. When using personal loans for debt consolidation, there are certain things to be careful of Your interest rate might increase later, and you may also extend the duration of your debt repayment. You should also steer clear of debt repayment strategies that are likely to cause more damage.

Strategies to Avoid When Paying Off Debts

When your focus is to increase your savings, you tend to search for the fastest ways to get rid of your debt. It is essential to accept that debt repayment may take a bit of time. Some of the methods you find are usually not the best in your situation. Here are some strategies you should avoid as much as possible:

Using Home Equity Loans

There is a massive problem if you must get a home equity loan to pay off your debts. It shows that you didn't consider the risks or search for better options. You can lose a lot if you take this route.

The main issue with the home equity loan is that the collateral, in this case, is your house. Some individuals will argue that they are expecting a windfall that will help in paying off the loan. What if this doesn't happen? What if there is no option to pay off the home equity loan? You run the risk of losing your house in the process, which just compounds your problems.

Debt Settlement

Debt settlement involves hiring a debt settlement company to help you reach an agreement with your creditor to reduce your debt. There are lots of reasons why this isn't a good idea. I recommend avoiding this option at all costs.

What is the guarantee that your creditor will agree to the terms the debt settlement company sets forth? There is no guarantee, and, in most cases, you end up aggravating your creditor. Is there a logical reason they should accept collecting less than what you owe?

Another issue is the additional debt you incur in the process. Some debt settlement companies may convince you to halt your debt repayment during the process. This means you are accumulating more debt with the hopes that they will be successful in their negotiations.

Tips That Can Help You Clear Your Debt Faster
Depending on your approach, you can reduce the duration of your debt repayment. This is beneficial if you want to avoid paying a lot of money as interest on the debt. Here are some simple tips to help:

Stick to a Budget
A budget is crucial if you want to get out of debt quickly. You need to create the budget and stick to it if you're going to be successful in your goal. The budget helps you control your spending, minimize expenses, and generate more money to pay off debts.

Don't Restrict Yourself to the Minimum Payment
It is convenient to diligently pay the minimum on your debts when working toward clearing it off. This is not an option if you want to clear the debt quickly and avoid paying too much interest. Your goal should be to allocate as much money as you can toward debt repayment. Use windfalls and any additional money to pay off the debt.

When you receive a bonus at work, the temptation to spend it on vacation or purchase something fancy will always be there. Don't give in; focus on what you intend to accomplish.

Enjoy the Benefits of Balance Transfers

As you learned earlier, using balance transfers is an excellent way to pay off your debt. It is essential to use it wisely. Push yourself to the limit and make it a goal to clear your debt before the end of the introductory period.

Avoid Accumulating More Credit Card Debt

If you have a credit card, the temptation to spend money you don't have will always be a problem. As you work toward paying off your debt, you must ensure you are taking steps to prevent adding on more debts. Don't let the rewards and cashback that you can earn fool you.

Cancel Automatic Credit Card Payments

If you aren't tracking your expenses accurately, then you will end up spending money you don't have. Subscriptions to various services may be set to renew automatically. You need to delete your details from sites that can automatically charge your account.

Sell Possessions to Earn Extra Money

In a later chapter, you will learn how to declutter to earn money. Selling some of your unwanted items can make you a substantial amount of money to assist in paying off your debt. The funds may not meet your minimum payment, but you can use it to cover essential expenses to prevent you from accumulating new credit card debts.

Make Changes to Your Lifestyle

Lifestyle changes include bad spending habits that will prevent you from making reasonable progress in getting out of debt. Any change you make should reduce your spending without negatively impacting your comfort.

Decluttering

The minimalism lifestyle requires a living space that is simple and free of clutter. This is when decluttering becomes necessary. Since you are likely going to be switching from the consumerist lifestyle to the minimalist lifestyle, there will inevitably be items you have accumulated over the years lying around.

Decluttering is the process of getting rid of these items. It focuses on removing the things that don't offer value in the home while retaining those that are useful. To get your home clutter-free, it can take as much as half a year. It is not a process that you can rush.

When you have time to declutter, you can be intentional in your actions during the process. Take time to decide what to keep and what to throw out. You can perform the decluttering process in steps. The first step is to quickly discard items that you are sure you will not need anymore. The next step involves making a conscious effort to observe the things you use and those that you don't.

You must get rid of those items during the third step of the decluttering process. There are various items in your home that you can get rid of. You can also sell these items for money during the process.

Investing

Once you start investing, you may notice one of your stocks is not performing well. Investing can be very exciting yet nerve-racking at the same time. It is not meant for short-term day trading but rather designed to grow your money for future lifestyle and expenses. Investing can be used to fund long-term goals such as college education, retirement, as well as short-term goals such as buying a car or house.

There are many ways to lose money from bad investments or expensive services; therefore, a large part of managing your investments should be about risk management and fee/cost management. Preservation of capital is key; it is usually better to take less risk even if the returns are lower. In a volatile market, a less risky investment can ease the stress that comes with losses.

There are also a lot of investments that have expensive fees associated with buying, selling, and managing them. You should never have to pay for most advice since there are so many free reputable resources on the internet, as well as several substitute investments that can save you on fee charges.

Starting on Investing

When starting to invest, as with any commitment, it is important to have a reason for buying or selling. Are you buying because someone is telling you to, or do you believe the investment will increase in value? Are you selling because you think the investment return is near the max, or have you found a better opportunity? There are many different scenarios to prepare for, but it is a good idea to have an entry and exit plan for each investment.

Inflation

To be successful at investing, the goal is to beat inflation. Inflation is the largest depreciation of investment returns since it decreases the value of your purchasing power over time and the number of goods you can buy in the future. Inflation varies as the economy fluctuates, but the general rule of thumb is that inflation is usually around 3-5% per year. Therefore, your investments should try to earn greater than the inflation rate of 3-5% per year.

Professional Vs. Individual Investing

Many academic books—and personal experience—have shown that professional investing services and advice rarely outperform a broad-based index fund. Professionals also tend to charge more fees for their services and will choose products that make them more money in commission than they make you in returns. An example would be a professionally recommended mutual fund with higher expense fees than an identical ETF.

Financial advisors tend to be salespeople that convince you of their company's professionally managed mutual funds. The portfolio manager picks and chooses stocks that mimic a particular strategy. Their trading is usually in response to market index changes; for instance, when a company becomes large enough to join the S&P 500, the mutual fund manager will have to mimic the change by buying that stock in the correct proportion. Your fees help pay the portfolio manager's exorbitant salary and other administrative costs. The craziness of the investment world is described in the below points;

- The market is efficient, and investing in a broad-based index fund will usually beat professional stock pickers over the long run.
- Stock prices, while not random, are supposed to be priced based on the company's fundamentals and future earning potential. All too often, they are mispriced and can cause disturbing trends or bubbles.
- There are many times when the stock market has artificially risen above its fundamental values (such as the dot com or housing bubbles recently) only to crash again. These short-term inefficiencies eventually crash, bringing the market back to more fundamental value.
- It is recommended investing in value stocks for the long term. It's all about the long run, and in the short term, stock picking is simply random.

Generally, it can be better investing yourself, as long as you study the market, stick to fundamentals, invest for the long term, diversify asset classes, keep your emotions and ego separate, and monitor costs. Before investing on your own, consult a trusted professional (non-sales) to see if going at it alone is the right thing to do for your situation. Psychology plays a large role in the investing world, and it's not always easy to stick to a plan since greed and fear tend to get in the way. Try to stick to the rules you have set for yourself and manage risk as much as possible.

Rebalancing and Diversification

Rebalancing means changing the proportion of investments you own in one asset class back to a particular percentage. For instance, if you are invested in four different funds, over time, some funds might make up a larger portion of your portfolio, which ties down the performance to that specific fund. Rebalancing means you might make the four funds equal to 25% each. Diversifying means that you might want to move more money into a higher-performing fund than another, or that you might want a larger portion of your portfolio in a real-estate fund and less in a large-cap fund.

Every six months to two years, it is a good idea to rebalance and diversify your investments to make sure you are properly allocating your assets. By rebalancing and re-diversifying, the portfolio will maintain acceptable risk and return levels and avoid the issue of too many eggs in one basket. This also applies to asset classes; for instance, you might not want all your investments in stocks, but instead, maybe some in bonds, real estate, etc.

Taxes

Taxes can also have a significant factor in your returns over time. When a mutual fund company sells stock in their fund, you might have to pay taxes at the end of the year if there was again. With an ETF, you are only charged when you sell the ETF. Tax laws might treat these events as capital gains or income depending on the scenario, holding period, and investment.

Additionally, tax laws treat short-term and long-term investments differently. A short-term investment is considered buying and selling within a 12-month time frame. Long-term is selling after a 12-month time frame. For most investments, short-term tax is treated at your income level rate while long-term tax is treated at the capital gains rate of 15 or 20%.

TRADING
Trading is different than investing in that you are much more active and engaged in the markets. It can be extremely frustrating or rewarding, but your ego will get the best of you unless you stick to solid trading rules. It's easy to think you're smarter than the markets, then make one bad trade, and lose everything you have recently gained. Knowledge, familiarity, experience, and back-testing are essential when trading.

It is important to only trade with extra money and not funds you plan on using for retirement or investing purposes. Trading profits should be used to enhance or quicken retirement, investment, and lifestyle goals. This means trading might speed up saving for a car, allow you to go on a vacation you have been putting off, or even retire a few years earlier!

When starting trading or investing account, try to open it with a minimum of $10,000. You can open a trading account with less, but it is not as effective. You might have to save up for a long time before you can open this account, but when you finally do, be extremely patient with using that money. Starting with this amount can help you get a better type of brokerage account, allow you better/more trading opportunities, and allow you to have enough liquid cash in case something burns through your emergency savings.

Some people still might open an account with $1,000-$5,000, but while they are limited, this allows them to do some conservative strategies and start learning.
Start with Investopedia.com for learning about these topics! They have great tutorials that set a foundation for investing. Constantly check Yahoo Finance for news, investing, and finding new opportunities. You can check quotes like EWZ and get a lot of information from their education center and investing tabs.

Stocks, Bonds, Futures, and Currencies
The primary market is the private ownership or initial buyers of an Initial Public Offering (IPO), which takes a privately-owned company public to where anyone can buy ownership in the company. When these initial owners sell their stock shares of the company, it sells on stock market exchanges, also known as the secondary market. The stock market is the place where investors come to trade stocks of just about every major company. When people say "stock market," they are referring to the secondary market.

A stock is partial ownership of a publicly owned company. Owning a company's stock allows you to participate in part of the company's profits or losses and might give you some voting rights in their business decisions. The amount of a company's stock, most individuals, own is usually not enough to make major business impacts since majority owners are usually considered over 5% of all outstanding shares of stock.

The broad stock market is made up of thousands of stocks and includes local stock exchanges in several regions around the world that large or small companies can trade on. Stocks can be grouped into sectors, regions, sizes, indexes, or anything else that is considered similar.

Bonds are traded similar to stocks, but they are a claim of a company's debt when it matures, instead of a claim on company profits. They also pay a coupon throughout the life of the bond, similar to a stock dividend. The common advice is to own a larger percentage of bond funds in your retirement portfolio, the closer you are to retirement.

Futures are more complicated to understand than stocks and bonds, but essentially, they are an agreement between the buyer and seller to buy a large amount of a commodity that the seller is producing. Imagine a wheat farmer selling a futures contract to a cereal maker. This helps lock in the price of the farmer's wheat at the financial risk of the cereal maker.

Other investors can speculate as to which direction commodity prices will go. Futures are highly leveraged, so any change in the price can affect your investment significantly. While considered riskier, futures are investments that can help stabilize and enhance a portfolio's performance.

Currency trading involves two different countries' currencies and the relationship between them. One country might have a stronger economy against another, so their currency might become stronger or weaker than the other. Companies mainly trade currencies to stabilize the price of their goods and investments in each country.

Mutual Funds Vs. ETFs
The common investing idea is to use mutual funds to grow your money. Mutual funds are a broad way to give an investor exposure to many stocks at the same time, making them great for diversification purposes. Most mutual fund accounts can also allow you to dollar-cost average your investments, meaning you can make monthly contributions instead of trying to time the market.

Most mutual funds will mimic the market but charge fees for this service, giving you a net return of 1-2% less than the market. Typically, these fees are for management, expenses, and sales commissions; a similar broad-based index fund or ETF will only have minimal expense fees in comparison.

The common substitute for mutual funds is an exchange-traded fund (ETF). An ETF is a basket of stocks or similar investments that can be traded the same way as a stock. The price of a mutual fund is updated and traded only once daily, while an ETF can be traded anytime the stock exchange is open.

These are some of the most common ETFs: the SPY (US S&P top 500 stock index), EWZ (Emerging Market fund - Brazil), VTWO (Russell 2000 Index), and much more broad-based ETFs. There are many other funds of developed countries' largest companies, small regional companies, and different types of emerging market ETFs like India and China. These are all designed for you to choose the funds that suit your investment needs and desires.

There are many companies that usually have low expenses charges for their ETFs. Some companies offer free commissions when you trade their specific ETFs. Instead of dollar-cost-averaging in a mutual fund (you can sometimes do this with as little as $25 a month), sometimes it makes sense to invest in an ETF, less often simple, but with more money, since the overall fees are less. You are still charged a small commission every time you buy or sell an ETF (similar to a stock commission), but with a mutual fund, you are charged higher annual expense fees and often upfront fees.

Be careful not to invest in too many different types of mutual funds or ETFs since each fund might have similar holdings. This would decrease the diversification benefits they are supposed to provide as a stand-alone investment.

Similar to the free ETFs, you can trade with individual brokers who have access to the same ETFs and can automatically rebalance and trade the account for you based on your risk tolerance and objective. It's a great way to make the trading part out of investing. The best part is you can deposit or withdraw whenever you want and with any amount for a normal account. These services are also great for IRAs and other retirement accounts.

General Trading Strategies

Buy and hold is the most common strategy for investing and retirement. The idea is to hold the stock or fund until you need access to the funds. In this strategy, it's important not to watch the prices go up and down daily as this is a long-term endeavor.

The market goes up and down each day, week, month, and year so some wait for deals in the market before entering a position. The reasoning is that it makes sense to wait until your price is favorable to buy (or sell), so you have a higher probability of positive or extra return. However, you mustn't miss opportunities by waiting too long.

Dollar-cost averaging is a concept whereby you don't actively watch prices to time the market for the most favorable entry and exit points, but instead, you invest regular amounts of money at regular intervals. This allows you to constantly stay invested without becoming frustrated if you missed some returns or entry points. The goal is to average out your buying points over time. You can add to this strategy by investing extra money during the short-term market declines.

It might make sense to scale in and out of positions to potentially capture profits along the way. This allows you to buy the stock or fund now, so you don't miss out on the upside potential in case it doesn't come down to the price you wanted. As long as you are comfortable/confident at your first buying point, any decrease gives you a better buying point with this mindset. This same concept should be used on the upside, so you capture some profits: sell some portion of the stock after you've achieved your desired return. Be conscious of tax considerations with this strategy since it will most likely count as short-term income tax.

Using limit orders is one of the best ways to get in and out of positions. A limit order tells your broker to buy the stock or fund at the price you specify instead of buying it at the current market price. This can allow you to take advantage of the intraday movements for your stock or fund. You can let those orders sit until they fill, or you can cancel the order after a period of time. With the market going up and down the way that it has, your limit order will most likely fill at the price you want soon enough; be patient with limit orders.

A good rule of thumb is to trade 100 shares at a time. This is called a lot of trade, so five lots would equal 500 shares. If you only start with a small account, you might not be able to buy 100 shares of a stock at a time. A lot allows you additional options such as easier selling and using stock options.

While these strategies are very basic in nature, they are enough to get anyone started. Once these are mastered, there is a plethora of strategies and philosophies in other books or on the internet that you can explore. There is enough literature out there to spend an entire lifetime learning about trading.

Chapter 6: Insurance Coverage

Health insurance might be the most important type of insurance since your health is what allows you to work and enjoy life. A simple hospice bill can get into a lot of regulation dollars. It is not worth risking getting into financial ruin while you try and save a few dollars on health insurance premiums. Many studies show that medical bills are the largest reason for personal bankruptcy. The majority of these situations are due to inadequate or non-existent health insurance coverage.

Additionally, with the transition of the U.S. Affordable Care Act, the health industry is going through a massive change, making it initially more complex. Luckily, it requires everyone to have health insurance; the U.S. government understands how expensive not having health insurance can be. Unfortunately, the Affordable Care Act puts the financial burden on insurance companies. Additionally, healthy lifestyles, pre-existing conditions, and unhealthy lifestyles are now on the same plan, further increasing the short-term costs.

Most developed countries have a universal, one-payer, health system which generally covers everyone and most situations. While universal insurance has its flaws, these countries have demonstrated it to be simpler, fairer, and less expensive than the U.S. healthcare system.

As mentioned previously, insurance through your employer is generally the cheapest. If you are between jobs, you can often get an individual short-term coverage plan or extend coverage with your previous employer. If you are under 26, you might be able to continue insurance under your parents' plan. If you are married, you may be able to receive coverage under your spouse's plan. If your employer does not offer health insurance or you are self-employed, you still need it.

Types of Health Insurance Plans
There are many different types of plans to choose from, but it is important to understand your options for each plan and choose the plan with choices/deductibles that fit your budget/situation. Some questions your health plan should answer are: who is your doctor, does the plan include dental care, vision care, prescriptions, and mail-order options, etc. Some people skip dental and vision because it doesn't fit into their budget, or they have lower needs for these items.

Life Insurance
Life insurance covers the costs associated with your death. As grim as this is to think about, life has value. Hence, it is necessary to have! The greatest reason for having life insurance ensure provision is there for those you leave behind.
This is extremely important if you have a family that is dependent on your salary. Death can cause lead to an income gap for your family, which can lead to financial trouble. Grieving is hard enough; dealing with financial issues associated with death can make things even harder.

Life insurance should be used to cover funeral costs, mortgage payments, loans, credit cards, taxes, living expenses, children's college, and give your family a financial cushion while they get back on their feet. The standard amount for a life insurance policy should cover ten times your yearly income. A good life insurance agent (while being salespeople) can help figure out your true need and what type of life insurance best suits you.

Types of Life Insurance
There are two basic types of life insurance: whole and term. Term life is the most common policy which gives you coverage for a set number of years at a relatively inexpensive premium. Whole life is a policy that never expires, has a cash value investment component, but is much more expensive than term. Both term and whole can have fixed or variable premiums, with the fixed option being most common.

At the end of the term life policy (usually 20 years), you can buy another policy, but at a much higher premium than your original premium due to your age. This can get very expensive later in life to where it might not be affordable (but also might not be necessary). The term is similar to auto insurance in that you hope never to use it, which means the premium payments are essentially "wasted" money.

Premiums for whole life can be about ten times as expensive as the term, but never increase and usually end at 65. The cash value and life insurance amount will continue to increase and payout when you die, no matter how old you are.

Term or Whole
Whole life is best bought younger in life since the premium payments are smaller and stay locked in

through age 65. The term is the cheaper option to cover all immediate insurance needs.

Many studies have shown that whole life insurance can be a waste of money, and people would be better off buying term and investing the difference. The idea is that instead of buying whole life, buy a term life policy and invest the money you would have spent on whole life into a retirement account. Unfortunately, this can be misleading since people generally do not have the discipline to actually invest what they would have spent on the whole life.

Whole life also has a cash value investment component that can give you a good, consistent rate of return and can be seen as a forced savings plan. Regarding the cash value, you can borrow against it, cancel the policy and collect it, or annuitize it at retirement while keeping most, or part, of the death benefit.

Having a baseline of whole life insurance, that grows over time, and supplementing the remaining needed expenses with term life seems to be the best way to manage a budget and maximize life insurance benefit.

Affordability and Legacy
Similar to health insurance, the most affordable option for term life insurance is generally your employer. You can only get a certain amount, and the coverage usually goes away if you leave or change jobs.

For additional coverage or whole life, find an agent of an insurance company and discuss their plans and options. Look into the stability of insurance companies, their cash value rate of return, and the cost of both types of insurance. Again, find a combination of whole and term that fits your budget while having enough coverage for your family's need.

Perhaps one of the best benefits life insurance offers is the legacy concept. If you've paid off your debt from the techniques described in this book, your beneficiaries probably don't need a ton of money, so why keep paying for millions of dollars in life insurance benefits?

Life insurance proceeds do not have to go solely to your family; they can also be used to support a charity you love. The donation from your death benefit can help decrease poverty or give food to those in need. It would be a neat consequence of your death that hundreds of other people can afford to live a better life! Your donation might be enough to build a new building or start a scholarship for your college. There are probably a million ways you can think of to leave a legacy, and life insurance can help.

After getting life insurance coverage, it is very important to have a living will so your beneficiaries have a plan for that money. This can also help avoid lengthy legal probate court issues. There are many cheap or free will/estate software/documents out there that only take a few minutes to complete.

Last four parts

Disability and Long-term care Insurance
Health insurance generally pays for more immediate care and hospital stays; however, it does not replace the income lost from being in the hospital, nor does it cover the costs of a nursing home. Disability and long-term care policies are designed to replace your income and cover daily expenses associated with your long-term disability.

Disability insurance usually guarantees 50-60% of your current income if you cannot work for a long period. While it does not cover all of your income, it can help cover expenses if you are faced with a devastating illness or injury. No one wants to become disabled, but any sort of accident can cause a disability, which makes this insurance so vital to one's financial future.

Long-term care insurance covers most costs associated with extended stay facilities (like nursing homes) and other house visits or living assistants. This covers diseases like Parkinson's and Alzheimer's, which affect a significant number of people. Unfortunately, long-term care is generally hard to buy under 45 years old.

Even people with great health insurance and a nice nest egg are never fully prepared for the time when they might not be able to work for weeks, months, or even ever again. Usually, when a disability occurs, your expenses increase by adapting to your new condition and lifestyle. This might include medical visits, altering your home and car, etc. These costs will be higher than your regular monthly costs before your disability, but 60% of your income is much better than 0%.

Many employers offer both short-term and long-term disability coverage as part of their benefits package, which would be the best option for securing affordable disability coverage. If your budget allows, seek out an insurance agent to get supplemental disability in order to cover up to 90% of your current income. If you are not employed or your employer does not offer disability insurance, seek out an insurer to cover the base 60% of your income and maybe a secondary insurer for additional coverage. The cost of disability insurance, as with most insurance, is based on many factors, including age, lifestyle, health, and family history.

Property and Auto Insurance
Property and auto insurance are usually mandatory when you own a home or vehicle. If you borrow money from the bank to finance these purchases, the bank will require insurance to protect their loan. Since a home is one of the largest assets a person might own, it is vital to adequately protect it against theft, fire, or weather disasters. In addition to the physical home, homeowner's insurance can cover the material possessions in the home, such as your TV, jewelry, etc.

Likewise, auto insurance covers issues related to the collision, property damage, personal injury, and liability costs associated with auto accidents. A vehicle is a high-speed heavy machine that can lose control and cause massive carnage and/or death if one mistake occurs.
The most common reason to have auto insurance is to cover the replacement of an expensive asset. If an

accident occurs and you do not have auto insurance, the only way to replace your vehicle would be to buy one from your savings. There is no reason to deplete your savings when auto insurance could cover these costs. If you, a passenger, or another driver is injured in an accident, your auto insurance will also pay for most or all of the medical expenses. It will also help guard you against any litigation that might result from the accident. Finally, auto insurance protects your vehicle against theft, vandalism, or natural disasters such as weather-related incidents.

Renters Insurance
If you rent instead of own, a renter's insurance policy is just as important. Your things in the apartment, or house, can add up to a significant amount of money. You might need to factor in a hotel or temporary relocation costs into the policy for some instances. Renters insurance usually costs about $20/month.

Since the 2007 financial crisis, property prices have actually decreased while rent has increased. This has created some interesting situations where owning can actually be cheaper than renting. The "American Dream" is usually to own, but the paradox is that one usually rents first in order to save up. In today's economy, it is easier to save money after owning an inexpensive condo rather than renting a similar apartment.

Insurance Tips
- Do some research into what **level of insurance** you have for each type of coverage and figure out what you think you

need. It's important to understand what your policy covers and what the deductibles are. The **minimum insurance** you should have will vary from person to person and is dependent on your financial situation. If you have other large assets or businesses, it is important to have significantly more than the minimum coverage amount to cover potential lawsuit costs.

- One way to **decrease your premium payments** is to increase the out of pocket deductible. This will require you to have the deductible amount saved up in case of an accident. You may also be able to lower your premiums by clearing up any bad driving records and having theft protection or good student discounts. Oftentimes, you can **bundle** your auto and home insurance to receive a discount on both.
- The overall idea behind insurance is **risk management**. This means you should try to decrease your lifestyle risk as much as possible. The healthier and safer your lifestyle, the cheaper most insurance premiums will be. Eating healthier, working out, driving safer cars or hybrids, obeying the laws, and generally being cognizant of safety can have a big impact on your wellbeing and bank account!

Chapter 7: Retirement Planning

Even if you have been diligently saving for retirement for years, you may be frightened of the financial pitfalls of health care in retirement. Remember, though, that there is still a great deal you can do over the next five years to save money on your health-care costs in retirement. You can either start saving money in a Health Savings Account or in a Roth IRA.

Abraham Maslow recognized safety as a fundamental human need and placed it in the second tier of the hierarchy of needs. Retirement security involves financial and psychological factors to ensure that an individual does feel safe or secure in the planning and ultimate experience of retirement. The main factor that we will focus on here is the financial one, which, when achieved, also allows an individual to fulfill the needs of psychological security.

Financial safety after retiring requires someone to plan and implement his or her ideas diligently before retirement. It involves saving up money or investing money to ensure that an individual will have something to live on after their work finally comes to an end in old age.

Investment is one of the best ways of preparing for retirement security, as it seeks to provide a person with profit in the future. Here, we are going to look at the type of mindset that an individual should have when investing for retirement. We will also see what passive income means, as well as the types of investments that an individual can have in it.

Retirement Security
Retirement security is the extent or level in which a person can comfortably provide a pre-retirement standard of living after retirement. Such an individual should live comfortably before retiring while making financial and psychological preparations for his or her life after retirement. Retirement security involves two aspects—financial and psychological security. Financial security refers to the money that an individual put aside via saving up or investing to spend it in retirement.

Psychological safety refers to the need to feel a sense that an individual does belong to society and that life will still be meaningful even after exiting the workforce. A person combines these two aspects to achieve retirement security. It enables him or her to feel secure, knowing that his or her life will carry on being significant as he or she gets older.

The Mindset on Investment for Retirement
Investment for retirement involves using money in the present to provide income in the future in post-employment. There are various mindsets that a person should have when dealing with investments for their retirement. These approaches offer an individual with guidelines that serve to manage risks relating to finances and allow them to make the best possible decisions. These mindsets include:

- **Conservative Attitude**

An individual should be more modest in what he or she chooses to invest in, along with the amount of investment he or she is willing to make. Older investors are close to retiring and thus invest in less risky stocks that pay higher dividends but are less volatile. An individual could also use mutual funds focusing on such securities rather than getting individual stocks. Additionally, investors, in regards to stocks, should always apply the rule of obtaining assets that weigh the same as the number that one gets when they subtract their age from a hundred. Thus, the older a person is, the less percentage in stocks they have, which, in turn, minimizes the risks involved while still allowing them to earn from the investment.

- **Cautious Mindset**

An individual should be careful in any investment that he or she makes. An individual should carry out extensive research in regards to the item or area in which he or she wants to invest. For instance, he or she should research and choose the best suitable account for high-interest account investment. Such an individual should be knowledgeable and fully understand the various concepts of investments such as annuities and what they entail before acquiring an annuity. These individuals must know the different elements of this investment and choose the ones that best satisfy their needs before obtaining an annuity contract.

A cautious investor should learn about volatile products such as bonds to know whether it will be a good or bad investment. A person should also be careful with their expenses: in that, he or she should always keep aside a certain amount of uncovered money in cash. This savings provides safety in that an individual will still have money even if he or she loses other investments in the economy and stock markets. A cautious mindset requires an investor to be conversant with everything associated with financing.

- **Taking Risks**

A person should also possess a risk-taking mindset, which he or she applies when he or she has a lot of income. Someone who has a lot of revenue can invest a considerable portion of it, which leads to him or her taking more risks. If successful, these investments enable the individual to grow and get more earnings, which will satisfy their needs in retirement and even extend to other beneficiaries around them. An individual should take these risks after careful considerations.

- **Being Simple**

A person should rebalance his or her portfolio by gradually switching to a more conservative one as they get older. Such an individual should also reduce the risks by focusing on a few separate funds for diversification. He or she requires minimum costs in terms of management and protect an investor from loopholes that can lead to significant losses in the investment process. They should also apply simplicity when taking risks, as this will enable them to make the most accurate decisions most efficiently and understandably.

Passive Income and Investing?
Passive income refers to the situation where individuals receive regular earnings after the work is over. The people here are not actively participating in the work and instead use minimal or no effort to earn money. However, it is essential to note that an individual must employ a lot of energy,

time, and money in the beginning before his or her investment can finally generate passive income.

Investing is a process through which a person produces future income. These individuals use the money to buy an asset, initiate or develop a project that will increase the worth of their money, and allow them to earn income in the future. The following are some of the areas in which a person can invest and obtain passive income, which, in turn, will result in a situation that would be described as "Earning money while sleeping."

Retirement is a fact of eventuality for every individual who is currently working on a business or organization where he or she is not the boss. For most people, earlier years of employment are characterized by an ability to hold down two or more jobs or put in extra hours in highly demanding jobs, in an attempt to make more money and live a comfortable life.

You could be one of those people who work so hard looking forward to the day you will finally get to hang up your boots and relax. You probably picture yourself at the end of your productive years, having settled down and enjoyed a serene life with your significant other by your side. You have probably dreamt about those years, how you will enjoy them free from the stress or anxieties of work. If all goes well, then the hustle and bustle you are currently engaging in will be over, and the rat race lifestyle you live now will be nothing but a memory.

However, retirement does not mean that your living expenses will miraculously disappear along with your anxieties. To maintain the living standards that you dream about and to have a decent quality of life during your retirement, you will need a reliable source of income.

In addition, in retirement, you will have grown older, and this means a lot will change physically and mentally. Having aged will mean that you will be prone to infections, traumatic injuries, and various other geriatric ailments related to advanced age. Your medical bills might end up costing much more than what you are spending now because, as an elderly citizen, your immune system will surely be a bit weaker. This means you will be more prone to illnesses that would be harmless to you today, or in general, when you were younger.

Therefore, as could be the case, finally getting off work and into retirement might not necessarily mean what you would have expected. You will still need to feed yourself well, to exercise in moderation to keep up your strength, to socialize to maintain your mental well-being, and of great importance, to preserve the ability to take care of your hygiene routine. It is with all these reasons in mind that a young and energetic working individual should already start mentally preparing for retirement. It is crucial to develop the skill of periodically investing a given fraction of your income thinking about your future retirement because you never know what tomorrow will have in store for you.

Conclusion

Finally, you need to take time for a budget review and track your progress in attaining your goals. Through review and tracking, you can quickly determine if you are deviating from your plan and solve any problems you come across.

Following these handy tips and acting will lead you to a better financial future where you will not only have more money, it will also give you peace of mind.

Thank You

I would like to thank you from the bottom of my heart for coming along with me on this journey. There are many books out there, but you decided to give this one a chance.

If you liked this book, then I need your help!

Please take a moment to leave an honest review of this book. This feedback gives me a good understanding of the kinds of books and topics readers want to read about and it will also give my book more visibility.

Leaving a review takes less than one minute and is much appreciated.

CPSIA information can be obtained
at www.ICGtesting.com
Printed in the USA
BVHW051158180821
614616BV00018B/1591